"Find the shortest, simplest way between the earth,
the hands, and the mouth."

—Lanza del Vasto, disciple of Ghandi

Tractor in the Pasture

RUSTING ICONS OF RURAL AMERICA

Lee Klancher

MOTORBOOKS
INTERNATIONAL

Dedication

To Dena Stehr
and Frieda Klancher

This edition first published in 2003 by Motorbooks International, an imprint of MBI Publishing Company, Galtier Plaza, Suite 200, 380 Jackson Street, St. Paul, MN 55101-3885 USA

© Lee Klancher, 2003

The information in this book is true and complete to the best of our knowledge. All recommendations are made without any guarantee on the part of the author or Publisher, who also disclaim any liability incurred in connection with the use of this data or specific details.

We recognize that some words, model names and designations, for example, mentioned herein are the property of the trademark holder. We use them for identification purposes only. This is not an official publication.

Motorbooks International titles are also available at discounts in bulk quantity for industrial or sales-promotional use. For details write to Special Sales Manager at Motorbooks International Wholesalers & Distributors, Galtier Plaza, Suite 200, 380 Jackson Street, St. Paul, MN 55101-3885 USA.

ISBN 0-7603-0876-4

Acquisitions Editor: Darwin Holmstrom
Project Editor: Peter Schletty
Designer: LeAnn Kuhlmann
Printed in China

On the front cover, top: A tractor abandoned on the plains of North Dakota.

On the front cover, bottom: A Pine Lake, Wisconsin farm.

On the frontispiece: This Massey-Ferguson rests on a central Wisconsin farm.

On the title page: A Farmall tractor on a ranch near the Colorado River in Utah.

On the contents page: A McCormick-Deering grain harvester in a ghost town in South Dakota.

CONTENTS

Weathered Iron and Good Light

Back in 1996, I was shooting a nicely restored Farmal tractor on a warm July evening. The front end of a rusty old McCormick-Deering was framed by poplar leaves and lit by the late light, so I snapped a couple of pictures. The resultant photograph is a favorite of mine, and I selected it as the lead photograph in my first book.

When the opportunity came to author a book of photographs of abandoned tractors, I immediately accepted the assignment. I enjoyed making the rusty McCormick image, and thought it would be good fun to photograph rusty old tractors as I traveled.

At first, I photographed every old tractor I saw. That soon proved to be counterproductive, as most old tractors abandoned to the weather are nothing more than old junk. The shots that caught my eye combined well-worn farms with beautiful landscapes. Add good light, and I found a recipe for photos that captured something special.

To find these images, I learned to look for farmhouses that hadn't been touched with a paintbrush in 20 years or more, with the paint peeled away and the siding turned gray by the sun, wind, and precipitation. When the owner lacks the time, money, or desire to keep a fresh coat of paint on the house, the yard is typically strewn with other evidence that the farm had seen better days: weathered, sagging barns, rusty windmills, and chicken coops buried in the weeds.

The other standard item on these farms is broken equipment. Everything from corn planters and combines to manure spreaders and milking machines take up residence in back lots, along fences, or behind the barn.

At places like these, I stopped, knocked, smiled, and asked if I could take some pictures. Some looked at me

quizzically and asked why, while others just shrugged their shoulders and nodded their heads. Others came out to show me around, or invited me in for coffee.

I've repeated this drill over and over during the past four years, visiting three continents and countless states. When I found that special blend of good light and gorgeous settings, I shot and, on occasion, was pleased with the film that resulted.

I discovered that an old tractor resting on a fencerow has a forlorn allure. My eyes were drawn to them as I drove by on the road. The more I photographed them, the more I came to enjoy sitting next to one in some godforsaken place and contemplating the fields and woods around it. I wondered about the people who had used this old tractor. What was their life like when that tractor was new? Why was the tractor abandoned to the elements? If machines could talk, old tractors could take us back to a time most of us can only imagine.

Part of the allure I find in these places is that they evoke childhood memories. I grew up in a farmhouse on the banks of the Brill River in northwestern Wisconsin. We were three miles from the nearest town, and the nearest kid was a half-mile down the road. As a young boy, I spent countless days on my own, fishing for crayfish in the river, hunting squirrels and rabbits in the woodpiles, and exploring the pastures and wooded river valley near our house.

Greenwood, Wisconsin

7

Middle Mound, Wisconsin

My grandfather spent countless hours sharpening lawn mower blades, oiling muskrat traps, and resuscitating old junk he brought home from the dump in this little shed he converted into his shop.

It was a lonely time—I can see that looking back now. But I was too young to know what loneliness really was, and those years instilled in me an understanding of the value of time spent on my own. I still prefer to hunt and fish alone, and need a bit of solitude in my life to feel whole.

So part of the allure of old tractors for me is the parallel I see between my own experiences and the state of that lonely old machine resting in a beautiful place. The solitary nature of the tractor's existence is a bit sad, but there are definitely days when I'd love to escape the hustle-bustle of modern life and spend my days with nothing better to do than contemplate a pasture.

Studying old tractors also evokes memories of my grandfather. He farmed for much of his life and had a Ford 9N on his farm in rural Wisconsin. In 1994, the scent of burnt oil and fuel that emanated from a running McCormick-Deering 10-20 brought back memories of my grandparents' place.

A gruff, generous man, my grandfather loved plowing snow, hunting deer, and his grandchildren. My memories of him are very fond, and I miss him keenly despite his being gone for more than 16 years.

Recollections of my grandfather and the parallel between an abandoned tractor and my childhood probably drive the longing, sadness, and comfort I find gazing at an old tractor in the pasture. For me, that old tractor is a lonely symbol of times past. Sitting in a field with that machine and admiring the sunset, I feel a bit of camaraderie with the old guy.

I also believe there are deeper, broader themes that these old machines draw out of our collective subconscious. There is something picturesque about a tractor resting in the pasture that almost anyone can see, and I believe an emotional response is evoked by that image.

The question I used as the basic thesis for this book was: Why do we feel this way? What in our common history, background, and cultural memory compels our fascination with old iron left for dead? This book is my answer.

—Lee Klancher
St. Paul, Minnesota
April 2003

Middle Mound, Wisconsin
This 9N put in 20 years of service hauling wood, deer, and maple sap on my grandparents' place. The engine is too worn to run, and the old machine has been replaced with a new Kubota.

CHAPTER 1

Indian Summer

"Cultivators of the earth are the most valuable citizens.
They are the most vigorous, the most independent,
the most virtuous, and they are tied to their country,
and wedded to its liberty and interests by the most lasting bonds."

—Thomas Jefferson, letter to John Jay, *The Papers of Thomas Jefferson*

The roots of rusty tractor magic go all the way back to the foundation of America, a country born on the backs of farmers and pioneers. The young nation's greatest resources were the vast tracts of land virtually untouched by European civilization, and the key to making that land useful was expansion.

In order for America to fulfill her manifest destiny, the frontier needed to be conquered. The battle to win the West would be fought with axes and plows rather than guns and swords. Starting with Thomas Jefferson, our pioneering leaders understood this. Jefferson commissioned Lewis and Clark to explore the West. A visionary, Jefferson celebrated the farmer and appeared to understand the role the farmer would play to use America's vast resources to make her one of the world's most powerful countries. The early American populace was encouraged to move west in the early 1800s. Land was given away, and ad campaigns urged people to pack up and take advantage of the open lands. "Go West, young man!"

No part of America's history has been as romanticized as the era of western expansion, from the canonization of early pioneers to the mythical allure of the Wild West's gun-toting heroes and villains. This period of our past is a fundamental aspect of American culture. The American ideals of self-reliance, independence, and respect for independent thought come straight from the westward expansion of the nineteenth century.

By the beginning of the nineteenth century, America's Manifest Destiny was mainly fulfilled. The West was won, and thriving towns and agricultural communities covered most of the country. The Native Americans had been pushed off the land and into reservations. The land was filled with farmers and ranchers stringing barbed wire fences, cutting forests, and breaking prairie.

Colorado High Plains

When the twentieth century dawned, America's ideals were young and fresh, but her future conflicted with those ideals. The country slowly became an industrial nation, and her people's way of life would change dramatically.

Farming was still widespread and prevalent, and the growing nation placed tremendous demands for crop production. Technology such as the reaper, the plow, and the advent of horse farming allowed the farmer to produce enough to make a good living. By 1890, a farmer could produce 100 bushels of wheat in about 40 to 50 hours, compared to the 250 to 300 hours required in 1830.

The farm in the early 1900s had kerosene light, balloon-frame housing, horse-drawn implements, and postal service. Nearly anything the farmer desired could be ordered through the Sears & Roebuck catalog, from schoolhouses and 11-room Victorian homes to guitar frets and the Heidelberg Electric Belt, which purported to enhance one's manhood through the joy of directly applied electricity.

In short, farm life was good in the 1900s.

There were, however, forces other than bizarre electrical devices at work changing the farm from its ideal state. The country remained predominantly rural in 1900, and nearly 30 million of the country's 76 million inhabitants lived on farms.

Closer examination of census figures shows that an interesting change occurred between 1850 and 1900. In 1850, 64 percent of America's workforce was farmers. By 1900, that number had shrunk to 38 percent. By 1950, farmers made up only 12 percent of the workforce. More Americans worked in factories, shops, and growing cities instead of on the farm.

One of the reasons for this societal shift was that technology allowed the farmer to improve his or her productivity. The reaper, plow, and the harvester were all machines that significantly improved farm yield.

The tractor, first introduced on the farm in the early 1900s, was one of the most important new tools. The significance of the machine was lost to all but the most observant because early tractors were clumsy, ill-behaved beasts.

Until about 1917, the tractor did not have a huge effect on the farm. The vast majority of farmers still used horses as the source of motive power, and tractor manufacturers felt the sale of a few thousand units a year was a success.

Henry Ford saw the potential of the farm tractor and understood that it could be an agent of change on the farm if it was affordable enough. He also understood that building tractors was a route to make real money. Ford introduced the Fordson tractor, a cheap, loud, and reasonably light machine. Through his massive dealer network, Ford sold a vast number of tractors.

The Fordson did not work terribly well. The rear drive system was cheap and heated the operator's backside almost intolerably. The drive systems also gave the Fordson the unfortunate propensity to rear up and flip over backwards, with less than desirable results to the operators who ended up underneath the heavy machine.

Despite the drawbacks, Ford sold large quantities of tractors and moved as many as 100,000 in a single year. More important, he made it clear to the farmer that a light tractor could replace the horse. He also forced the industry to produce a light tractor at a reasonable price.

The ironic part of the Fordson story involves the dangerous little machine's impact on American life. Ford's light tractor ultimately spelled the end of the Golden Age of farming. As mechanization came to the farm, the farmer was able to produce more crops. Fewer farmers were required to feed America, and the country's rural lifestyle would truly end. Just as the Fordson tractor killed untold numbers of operators when it flipped over backwards, it also killed an ancient way of life. As the leading edge of the industrial revolution's move to the farm, the Fordson was the harbinger of doom for rural America's glory days.

What is it that draws our eyes to rusting Fordsons in the fields and fencerows? In those rusty flanks, our cultural subconscious may conjure an idealized way of life long gone. Some part of us longs for the days when the guy at the general store knew our names and people on the street asked about our new baby or broken wagon axle.

If you look deeper, you'll find the faded shadows of the western ideal, the concept that we have to work up the courage, pick up the family, and move west in order to make our dreams come true.

Perhaps you'll simply find this ideal a few miles from home, in the way rusty iron looks in the soft light of a fading fall day. Whatever form the attraction takes, the roots of our agrarian past live and breathe in these rusty icons of rural America.

"The premise of the American West has always been that there's another West lying just over the horizon, a place to annul the past, to reoriginate. That premise was never really true, but it was a way of making sense of such a vast quantity of land."

—Verlyn Klinkenborg, *The Rural Life*

Willard, Wisconsin

"The sign might be as innocuous as a continuous expanse of fields where the buildings of an earlier farm once stood, or as arresting as the vacant gaze of an abandoned homestead, choked with weeds and falling to ruin. Traveling across this landscape, it is not hard to imagine what it will look like when there is only one farmer left."

—Kathryn Marie Dudley, *Debt and Dispossession: Farm Loss in America's Heartland*

Willard, Wisconsin

15

Homesteading

By James M. Cesnik, from "Ignac Cesnik—Land Agent,"
Spominska Zgodovina

[Ignac Cesnik] came to Willard as a land agent in the winter of 1907–08, and after moving his own family into the bunkhouse of an abandoned logging camp a few miles to the north of what was to become the village of Willard, he persuaded scores of his fellow Slovenian immigrants that they could find in the same area the 'good life' they were seeking for a minimum investment of money and a little hard work.

"The first part was certainly true, even by the standards of that time. Selling price of this land was $4 an acre; $160 for 40 acres (the most popular-sized parcel); $10 down and $10 a month at 6 percent interest. . . .

"The second part—a little hard work—was perhaps something of an understatement. For while there were thriving, established farms, villages, towns, and cities nearby . . . the area around Willard was a pocket of raw wilderness. It required the most arduous, bone-wearying toil to convert it to farmland. It had been cut over by the N.C. Foster Lumber Co. of Fairchild for stands of virgin pine and white oak, but was still covered by the stumps and substantial stands of maple, basswood, birch, ironwood, and more. It was accessible only by foot, horseback, or horse-drawn vehicle across rudimentary trails or—the best access—via N.C. Foster's Fairchild and the Northeastern Railway.

"Ill fares the land where men decay."

—Rural Folklore

Nameless Backroad, Central Wisconsin

Old Mining Road, Nevada
The Union Pacific, along with the Central Pacific, helped open the American West with the completion of the transcontinental railway. This surprisingly well-preserved boxcar is a reminder of the Union Pacific's pioneering contributions.

Opposite:
The Road to Moab, Utah
I was coming back from a mountain biking trip with my friends, Dave and Laurel, and a hyperactive lab, Buddy, when this planter was spotted. I'm not a big fan of implements as lawn ornamentation, but the colors, setting, and light were too good to pass up.

Virgin Prairie

By I.G. Haycraft
From "Breaking Prairie," *Stored by Minnesota Historical Society*

There is something about a broad expanse of virgin prairie that is hard to describe adequately. It is sensitive to weather condition and responds to and marks the seasons, spring, summer, autumn, and winter. Grass starts to grow soon after the warm days of spring have arrived, and as the season advances, the grass is interspersed with a profusion of wild flowers, portraying nature at her best. It is well nigh impossible for anyone who has not viewed such a scene to properly understand the wonderful beauty of it. . . .

In the early days, a large percent of the prairie was burned over after frost had killed the grass, etc., and the Breaking Prairie season begins as soon as the new growth of grass is well started in the spring. The particular section of Minnesota where I spent the first 30 years of my life, all the breaking I did personally was done chiefly with a 4-horse team, hitched abreast. I have done a little breaking with 2- or 3-horse teams and smaller plows, and I have seen plenty of tractor Prairie Breaking outfits. I have probably walked in the furrow made by a 16- or 18-inch Breaking Plow hauled by 4 good horses while breaking somewhere around 1,000 acres from first to last, covering a period of years until there was no more real virgin prairie left to break in this location. The Prairie Breaking process is almost like any other enterprise. There is one real right way to do it for best all around results and it is like many other kinds of work that has changed a lot as the years go by, and the use intended for the fresh upturned sod. In the very early days in southeastern Minnesota, the farmers did not attempt to grow any kind of crop on freshly broken prairie sod. It generally was allowed to lay exposed to the weather all through the summer months and in the late fall, furrows were turned back with grass side up and left to lay in such condition until spring weather when it was processed by harrow or disk to make ready for spring wheat, to be sown as early as season would permit.

Rogers, Minnesota

Somewhere in Utah

The Thresher Comes to Call

By I.G. Haycraft
From "Threshing," *Stored by Minnesota Historical Society*

Along about 10 A.M., we sighted the machine approaching from the north and a little bit west. Bear in mind, at this early date, there were absolutely no roads. It just a matter of picking your way over the prairie, dodging sloughs and crossing creeks at the most favorable place. Those Bundys were good at it. They were typical pioneers. Oh, what a majestic procession this outfit made as they came nearer. The separator was hauled by a yoke of very large red oxen (some years later replaced by a team of mules) driven by Willis Bundy. The old gentleman Bundy, the father, was some distance ahead looking the ground over for the best course to follow. Immediately behind the separator was Bert and his yoke of steers, hauling the trap wagon loaded with all the needed equipment, and following Bert was George with another yoke of oxen, hauling the horsepower.

*"There is a cloud on my horizon.
A small, dark cloud no bigger than my hand.
It's name is progress."*

—Edward Abbey, *Desert Solitaire*

Outskirts of Moab, Utah

23

North of Green Bay, Wisconsin

Steam Power

Farmer W.J. Hastings of Wapakoneta, Ohio, 1877, from
***The McCormick Engines* brochure**

The ten-horse traction engine that I bought from you last summer did all that you claimed it would do. It went through good and bad roads all the same, and hauled the water tank on all kinds of roads. We had a great deal of rain and very bad roads in this part of the country this fall, but our horses had nothing to do but to guide the engine. We saved time in not having to double teams on our engine. Some steam-threshermen had to put three teams on their engines, without their tanks, when the roads were bad, while we could take the engine and tank over the same roads with one team, and it would not have to pull any. I would not have an engine without the traction on it.

Australian Outback

I shot this McLaren portable steam engine one afternoon during a motorcycle trip. Several years later when I contacted a club in Leeds, UK, to look for information about the machine, they told me it very well might be the last portable McLaren in existence. The machine has since been moved into preservation.

"*Whenever people learn to become self-sustaining on farms or in small rural communities, then industry will seek out these communities. Industry will follow people to the smaller towns and many of our problems will be solved.*"

—Henry Ford, "$5 a Day Basic Wage for Ford Workmen," *Ford News*, April 1934

North of Seattle, Washington

The Ozarks, Arkansas
Farmers who searched for power on the farm on occasion converted automobiles to suit their needs. Skilled welding and scrounged parts converted this Chevrolet to provide belt power.

"In the fall, Dad was plowing with a 1923 Fordson, and the weather was getting cold.
He would drain the radiator at night, and would build a fire under the oil pan in the morning
to warm it up so it would start."

—Donald L. Price, "Rollin' Up the Drive Belt: The Story of My Life Pertaining to Machinery,"
Engineers & Engines

Central Wisconsin

29

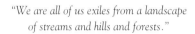

*"We are all of us exiles from a landscape
of streams and hills and forests."*

—J.B. Jackson, *Ghosts at the Door*

Sonoma Valley, California

"We had a Fordson for our first tractor.
It was a screamer. It made so damn much
noise you had to wear earplugs.
You could hear it for forty miles."

—Clyde Berkshire,
farmer and tractor collector

**Sonoma Valley Pumpkin Patch,
California**

CHAPTER 2

A Long, Cold Winter

"Burn down your cities and leave our farms, and your cities will spring up again as if by magic; but destroy our farms and the grass will grow in the streets of every city in the country."

—William Jennings Bryan, campaign speech,
Democratic National Convention of 1896

The Depression began on the farm long before Wall Street bankers jumped from windows on that fateful day in October 1929. In fact, it began in 1921, as times turned hard for farmers. A chilling mix of poor farming practices, dwindling prices, economic collapse, and natural catastrophe left farmers destitute, penniless, or bankrupt.

As the light faded on the farm, America's growing urban population experienced a moral revolution. The roaring 1920s saw a fundamental conflict in values driven by the industrial revolution. The rigid moral code that structured the fundamental values of America was challenged, chastised, and abandoned in favor of a celebration of debauchery and the easy pleasures of the nouveau riche. As the farmer watched his or her way of life crumble during the droughts of the mid-1930s, urban America cavorted with the luxuries of a newfound way of life. This period was a flamboyant challenge of the agrarian ethic by a society that embraced the new ethos created by an industry-driven culture.

While the growing urban segment of America cavorted with the newfound joys of commerce, the farm faltered. During and immediately after World War I, demand for American agricultural products increased worldwide. Farmers responded by opening up more land and adding new equipment (and, on occasion, mounting debt). Land values doubled and tripled, and farmers went through a relatively prosperous era.

Beginning in 1921, the improved days on the farm ended. The overseas demand for American agricultural products dried up as politicians imposed strict import tariffs. When European countries responded with tariffs of their own, America found itself with an abundance of agricultural machinery that was able to produce more than the country required.

The result of overproduction was lowered crop prices. To compensate for the lower prices, farmers had to produce more in order to make a respectable living. Meanwhile, the farm equipment manufacturers rapidly developed new implements to help the farmer be more efficient and produce more crops. A nationwide lust for capital compounded the lust for equipment. Giant corporations required more and more profit to stay afloat, and they went after it with guns blazing.

The most significant player in the farm industry was the International Harvester Company (IHC), which was formed at the turn of the century when the giants of the agricultural equipment industry merged. This young conglomerate became the Big Brother of the agricultural world in the first 20 years of the twentieth century. IHC bought up twine manufacturers, steel plants, and competitors with the goal of owning the process of building machinery from the forge to the dealerships.

Henry Ford's affordable Fordson was a huge upset for the growing behemoth that was IHC. The cheap little machine sold in volumes that IHC executives could only dream about. As a result, IHC began a massive engineering effort to use its vast company resources to create an effective tractor that could replace the horse. Its company-wide efforts came up with the McCormick-Deering 15-30 and 10-20, which were little more than a better-engineered version of the Fordson.

Fortunately for IHC, one of its engineers, Bert Benjamin, had been working on a revolutionary concept that was exactly what the market demanded. In the mid-1920s, IHC introduced the Farmall tractor and found the gold mine they had sought. The tractor was a huge success. Farmers bought the new machines, and their horses became limited-use pasture trimmers, pets, and prospects for the glue factory.

The supreme irony of this act was that although it played a role in the farm's transformation from an American way of life to another form of small business, it also played a significant role in the demise of the farm. Farmers who bought the machines were rewarded with increased output to accompany the increased debt necessary to buy the tractor. The farmers continued to overproduce, and prices continued to drop.

The only possible way for this system to function properly was to eliminate the weaker and less profitable farms so the production could level out and meet the demand.

The result was that the machine of industry destroyed the agrarian way of life. This problem was widely recognized as early as 1870, and the plight of the farmer was shouted from the rooftops. This plight was more than an ordinary business change—it was the death of a national way of life.

In the 1920s, American's agrarian way was also challenged by rapidly changing values. Bolsheviks sent letter bombs, and the labor movement struggled to bring reasonable wages to the lower class. President Woodrow Wilson poured his soul into the formation of the League of Nations. Back home, the Red Scare blossomed and the Ku Klux Klan rose in power. Prices rose, rent increased, and women wore shorter skirts (six inches above the ground!).

This change did not come easily. On September 16, 1920, a large bomb was set off at the corner of Broad and Wall Street in New York City. The corner hosted the law offices of J. P. Morgan and the New York Stock Exchange. Thirty people were killed and hundreds were injured. The intersection was enveloped in a hail of rising dust and falling glass. A milling mob scene of the dead, wounded, and would-be helpers fumbled through the dust. The explosion ignited the Red Scare and gave the American public a terrifying event that lent credence to the ludicrous idea that the communists were going to take over.

As the Red Scare passed, the next fear du jour was the younger generation's apparent lack of moral conviction. They were smoking (even the women!) and listening to vulgar music. The dancing was close and suggestive, and casual sex was considered morally acceptable by some.

Guardians of American morality reacted swiftly to these challenges to the American way. In 1925, the citizens of Norphelt, Arkansas, passed an ordinance that outlawed sexual intercourse within the city limits. If the couple was married, an exception could be made. If the act was "of a grossly improper and lascivious nature," then the couple—married or not—could be arrested and prosecuted for violating this city order.

The plight of the farmer was nearly overshadowed by these changing times. While farm prices plummeted, the suburbanites of the world tuned in to the Jack Dempsey fight or *Amos 'n' Andy* on the new national past time, the radio. They took their new Ford Model Ts down to the chain grocery store to shop or to the theater to catch the latest Charlie Chaplin or Clara Bow film. The wonders of the industrialized society were coming home. The eyes of the nation were turned to the new wonders of the Industrial Age, and the style of the decade was decidedly urban. These styles and tastes made it to small towns all across the country. The agrarian ideal the country was founded on was not terribly prevalent in the 1920s.

By the close of the decade, however, the farm's problem spread to the rest of the world with the Great Depression. As the plight of the farmer became the woes of a nation mired in hard times, the fickle interests of the public once again focused on the farm. The transition from the roaring 1920s to the Depression of the 1930s was a crisis for the farm and for American values.

When the situation on the farm turned from bad to worse in the early 1930s, farmers struggled to make ends meet. Overextended farmers saw banks reclaim their property, and families were turned into vagabonds and gypsies. John Steinbeck wrote about this, first in a series of newspaper articles, and later in his celebrated novel *The Grapes of Wrath*. He painted a picture of destitution that was sympathetic to the plight of migrant farmworkers.

In 1936, an editor at *The San Francisco News* assigned Steinbeck to write a series of articles about the dust-bowl migration in rural California. Steinbeck spent the summer visiting the state's agricultural valleys in an old bread truck. What he discovered was that the workers who lived on the road and traveled from farm job to farm job were displaced farmers. His sympathetic portrait of them, both in the articles and later in his novel, helped the country see and understand the farmer's troubles in a more empathetic fashion.

"The drought in the middle west has driven the agricultural population of Oklahoma, Nebraska, and parts of Kansas and Texas westward. Their lands are destroyed and they can never go back to them. Thousands of them are crossing the borders in ancient rattling automobiles, destitute and hungry and homeless, ready to accept any pay so that they may eat and feed their children," Steinbeck wrote in one of his articles.

Interestingly, the farm depression of the 1920s and 1930s did not drive as many people from the farm as one might expect. Nearly one million farmers left in that period, but that made up only about 2.5 percent of the total number of farms in existence. This was nearly insignificant compared to the nearly 50 percent reduction in number of farmers between 1950 and 1960.

Life on a farm during the Great Depression was difficult, but the Depression did not actually destroy the farm in America. What it did was draw attention to the troubles of the farmer during a time when the entire nation struggled with its economy, values, and changing way of life.

Outskirts of Stillwater, Minnesota

"Agriculture was poorly coordinated in the national life and moved painfully along from crisis to chronic depression, a dangerously sick industry in an otherwise thriving decade."

—James H. Shideler, *Farm Crisis 1919–1923*

Collector's Personal Scrapyard, Clear Lake, Wisconsin

Central Wisconsin

Clear Lake, Wisconsin

Monticello, Minnesota
This Farmall tractor was buried in the grass behind a collector's house. I found it while photographing a nicely restored Farmall for my first book. The late evening light was nice, and the resultant photo was one of my favorites.

40

"Here was a new generation . . . grown up to find all Gods dead, all wars fought, all faiths in man shaken."

—F. Scott Fitzgerald, *This Side of Paradise*

Black Hills, South Dakota

41

Black Hills, South Dakota

"Society never advances. It recedes as fast on one side as it gains on the other."

—Ralph Waldo Emerson, *Self-Reliance*

Central Wisconsin

Somerset, Wisconsin

On a warm summer evening, I took my camera and went for a drive down the dusty backroads near my rental place on Pine Lake. This old John Deere was surrounded by junked bicycles, chopper boxes, and farm equipment. The bird's nest caught my eye as a sign of life in this otherwise desolate boneyard.

"For a transitory enchanted moment,
man must have held his breath
in the presence of this continent,
compelled into an aesthetic contemplation
he neither understood nor desired,
face to face for the last time in history
with something commensurate [with]
his capacity for wonder."

—F. Scott Fitzgerald, *The Great Gatsby*

Colorado River Valley, Utah
Utah is one of the most photogenic places
I know, and finding this old Farmall in
such a striking setting was a nice surprise.
Old tractors are not terribly plentiful
in this part of the world, where farms
are few and far between.

45

Chippewa River Valley, Wisconsin
*This Massey-Harris shows signs of a
farmer's ingenious battle to keep old
machinery working with homespun repairs.*

"As the householder evolves into a consumer, the farm evolves into a factory—with results that are potentially calamitous for both."

—Wendell Berry, *The Unsettling of America*

Central Wisconsin

Rocky Mountain Foothills, Colorado

Monticello, Minnesota

50

Eastern Wisconsin

South Dakota

The Plains states were hit particularly hard by the farm depression of the 1920s and 1930s. This McCormick-Deering has become part of a South Dakota field.

Just Off Highway 89, Southern Utah

I found this Farmall F-20 in a yard full of junked cars and tractors in Utah. The owner of the yard was installing a rebuilt engine into a battered old car when this photo was taken.

North Dakota Badlands

54

"A bone is the evidence of life—a life
unique, unprecedented,
and never to be repeated, which,
though it has vanished, nevertheless
endures in the bone;
a faint white glimmering, in some
offhand place, of life everlasting."

—Paul Gruchow, *Bones*

Clark County, Wisconsin

Coon Fork, Wisconsin

"For if a man farms his land to the waste of the soil or the trees,
he destroys not only his own assets but Nature's assets."

—Franklin Delano Roosevelt, State of the Union Address, 1938

Eastern Farm Country, Wisconsin

*"After the forest came the pasture,
and the pasture in time became the lawn…
Our lawns are merely the civilized
descendants of the medieval pasture
cleared among the trees."*

—J.B. Jackson, *Ghosts at the Door*

St. Croix River Valley, Minnesota

CHAPTER 3

Hope Springs from the Ashes

"We must build a new world, a far better world—one in which the eternal dignity of man is respected."

—Harry S. Truman, Address to the United Nations Conference in San Francisco, April 25, 1945

When 1939 arrived, America was coming out of the Depression and would soon enter World War II. These two forces collided and drew the country out of the difficult process of rebuilding and into a new role as the world's sheriff. Rural America entered a second revolution as it attempted to feed the world through mechanization and increased production.

The government's role and attitude toward agriculture shifted fundamentally. In the 1920s and even the early 1930s, the government's efforts to help the farmer were focused on education, loans, and "weed-out" programs designed to force the farmer to treat his or her way of life as a business. Beginning in 1940, this "live or let die" attitude increased the farmer's dependence on subsidies and programs designed to encourage the farmer to produce less and treat the land in environmentally friendly ways.

61

Perhaps the Depression showed the leaders of the day that leaving the farm to its own devices could be disastrous for the economy. By 1940, more than six million farmers received federal subsidies. International markets were reopened with free-trade agreements, and the Farm Security Administration subsidized loans and offered attractive refinancing terms for farmers.

The effect of these programs was positive. Farm prices increased and production stabilized. Farming became a more viable option, and the farm population actually increased slightly between 1930 and 1940.

Other programs, such as the Rural Electrification Act, were designed to bring modern conveniences to the farm. Despite the growth of modern technology on the farm, the wonders of the Industrial Age were still a bigger part of suburban life. In 1940, only one-third of American farms had electricity, and only a quarter of them had telephones. More than half had cars, which was a testament to Henry Ford's vision to put the common man on wheels.

While governmental and economic forces improved the farm situation, the farm wasn't truly transformed until World War II. America put an incredible amount of resources into the war, once it decided to participate, and that meant many of the men who did the work on the farm, owners and hired hands alike, were sent overseas to fight.

A nationwide demand for manpower, either to fight the war overseas or to build the machines and supplies of war domestically, found a place in society for the sharecroppers who were brought to the cultural eye by John Steinbeck and the Depression-era photographers. In addition, the war and the improved international trade situation increased the demand to produce on the farm.

Low manpower and high demand forced the farmer to become more efficient. Almost without exception, the answer to that problem was mechanized farming. From 1940 to 1954, agricultural manufacturers sold the largest volume of tractors in American history, and the move to farm mechanization was completed in this time period.

In 1954, for the first time in American history, tractors outnumbered horses on the farm. The agricultural equipment industry's dream to replace animal power was realized as the tractor became an effective, viable machine.

The soundness of the tractors built in this era can be seen with a quick drive through a rural community today. The tractors of the 1940s and 1950s can still be found working hard in the fields of small farms and the yards of hobby farms. These machines are, on occasion, used simply because the farmer can't afford better equipment. In other cases, the use of a 50-year-old tractor is a conscious choice. These machines are still effective, and their durability is legendary.

Back in 1954, horse farming was still a fixture on small or very poor farms. Just as some of today's farmers use old Farmall Ms or Allis-Chalmers WD-45s, a segment of farmers chose to stick with horses. The connection between the farmer and his or her animals was a multifaceted thing. Some farmers view their animals as property rather than living creatures, and the relationship can be a bit dismaying to urban dwellers accustomed to seeing animals as wonders of nature, entertainers of children, or household members. Still, there are farmers who cherish the connection with horses, mules, or oxen. There is certainly a natural resonance that comes from farming with draft animals. The fields they work provide fuel, and the animals' manure, in turn, provides fuel for the fields.

Nostalgic methods aside, the industrial revolution had truly arrived on the farm by 1954. Along with the tractor, rural America was discovering the conveniences of modern society. By 1950, electricity was prevalent on the farm, with 93 percent of American farms hooked up to the nation's power grid. Just shy of half had telephones, and about three-quarters had automobiles.

Farm population was on the decrease in the 1940s and shrank from 30.8 million in 1940 to 25.1 million in 1950. With the U.S. population on the rise, this meant that the percent of the country that made its living by farming decreased statistically from 18 percent in 1940 to 12 percent in 1950. Considering that farmers made up 64 percent of the population in 1850, there was a dramatic shift in the populace over this tumultuous period.

When the war came to a close, the postwar boom hit the farm and things continued to improve in terms of production and profitability. Tractor sales after the war were astonishing, and the manufacturers focused their efforts to obtain ample iron, rubber, and other essential materials to meet the demand for their products. The government maintained strict control of the war-depleted supply of these materials, and year-end reports from executives at the ag industry companies were filled with pleas for more material and complaints that they could not meet the demand for their machinery. The technology they produced revolutionized the farm, and the companies knew the time was ripe to reap the benefits.

The time was a good one to be part of the workforce, and an average salary for an honest day's work was enough to support a family and enjoy all the modern conveniences. The allure of this lifestyle drew people off the farm in significant numbers.

One of the most significant modern conveniences to appear in this era was television, which saw widespread acceptance in the postwar boom. In any discussion of the lost ways of our past, television most certainly has a role. Whereas information at the turn of the twentieth century came to people primarily through the newspapers and word of mouth, the prime source of almost every piece of information that the culture shared in the latter half of the century would come from television.

Despite the decrease in rural populations, agricultural production increased due to a higher demand and improved technology. The rise in frozen food and international markets drove up demand, and times once again became reasonably prosperous for the farmer. These changes in the farm pushed the rural ideals further from the American reality as the suburban ideal became the dominant way of life. Even the farmer's idealized lifestyle was changing. Farming was a business that was the choice of fewer and fewer Americans.

The ideals of the pioneer farmer lived on, and had perhaps even been adapted to the suburban ideal. The concept of working hard and making your own destiny remained a powerful force in American values. The idealized view of reality in the 1950s may have been an attempt of the postwar culture to put aside the recent wounds of a costly (albeit victorious) war and the bitter depths of the Great Depression. Life in the 1950s was good, and America dearly wanted to believe that.

Happiness in America, once thought to be found in the ideals of self-denial and a spare lifestyle, was being pushed aside by the needs of an increasingly commercial society that encouraged Americans to buy the latest gadget. A hard life full of long days of work and simple pleasures had been replaced with *Leave It to Beaver*.

Mississippi River Valley
That curving line over the logo was penned by famed industrial designer Raymond Loewy.

Left and far left:

Foothills of the Cascade Range, Washington

While I photographed these Fergusons, my friend Anna Wheeler talked with the woman living on the farm. The woman told Anna that her family had been living on this farm for more than 100 years, and that the existence had been a struggle. The family was considering selling the farm, but didn't have the heart to leave the land that they loved.

Nevada Plains

Chippewa River Valley, Wisconsin

I found this Minne-Mo behind an old farm. I stopped and knocked on the door, and an old farmer came out and showed me around the place. He had old tractors everywhere, buried in junk cars, abandoned equipment, and weeds.

Chippewa River Valley, Wisconsin

Black Hills, South Dakota

"The nation that destroys its soil destroys itself."

—Franklin D. Roosevelt, letter to state governors, urging soil conservation laws, February 26, 1937

Connorsville, Wisconsin

Foothills of the Appalachian
Mountains, Virginia

"It is difficult to describe the rapacity with which the American rushes forward to secure the immense booty which fortune proffers to him . . . . They early broke the ties which bound them to their natal earth, and they have contracted no fresh ones on the way."

—Alexis de Tocqueville, *On Democracy*

Southern Wisconsin

North Dakota Badlands

The North Dakota Badlands are one of the most beautiful places I know. Teddy Roosevelt established a national park here. My friend and editor Darwin Holmstrom introduced me to the gorgeous rugged country of the Badlands on an off-road motorcycle ride. The big sky, rolling buttes, and open grassy expanses will bring me back. A thick, cheap steak and cold draft beer at a local tavern confirmed Darwin's and Roosevelt's high esteem of the area.

North Dakota Badlands

Just off Interstate 90, South Dakota
*I came across this ghost town on the way
home from a Colorado motorcycle trip.
Crossing the Great Plains on a motorcycle
was a rite of passage for me as a young
man, just as it was a rite of passage for
the pioneers of young America. Even
back then, South Dakota was mostly
a "just passing through" state.*

Company Yard Ornament, Iowa
The International TD line of crawlers once carried the hopes of a powerful company. The company has been merged into near oblivion, and this crawler has become a lawn ornament.

"I've heard people say that World War II
really proved something.
The main thing it proved to me was
how long my dad . . . and many others
like him could keep machinery running
after it was already worn out."

—Donald L. Price, "Rollin' Up the Drive Belt:
The Story of My Life Pertaining to
Machinery," *Engineers & Engines*

Extraterrestrial Highway, Nevada
*When America joined World War II, the
country's manufacturing machine built
tanks, half-tracks, and guns. This truck
rests not far from Area 51.*

Wine Country Pumpkin Farm,
California

Desert Home, Nevada

"That one American farmer can now feed himself and fifty-six other people may be, within the narrow view of the specialist, a triumph of technology; by no stretch of reason can it be considered a triumph of agriculture or of culture."

—Wendell Berry, *The Unsettling of America*

Colorado High Plains

Treasure County, Montana
Clarke Sutphin photo

Australian Outback

This tractor was spotted by my friend Warwick Schuberg, a gregarious Australian motorcycle tour company owner. I was on tour with Warwick and about a dozen others and rode the foul stretch of road that runs up Australia's crocodile-infested northeastern coast to Pijinka, a city-block-sized hunk of granite that is the northernmost point in Australia. On a 100-plus-degree day, Warwick stopped the group of bikes and yelled back to me, "Tractor!" He knew I was working on a book and kept his eyes open for old tractors. While the group sat and baked in the Outback sun, I grabbed some photos of this Farmall M and an old church.

Australian Outback

"*But when it does, he adds philosophically—when the last farmer's tractor breaks down—the land will revert to wild prairie, the frontier will be opened for resettlement, and the pioneering cycle will begin anew.*"

—Kathryn Marie Dudley, *Debt and Dispossession: Farm Loss in America's Heartland*

Colorado High Plains

Near Sarpy Creek, Montana
Clarke Sutphin photo

Central Wisconsin

Central Wisconsin Ghost Farm

Wisconsin Ghost Farm

"If we want the land to be cared for, then we must have people living on the land who are able and willing to care for it."

—Wendell Berry, *Another Turn of the Crank*

Wisconsin Pasture

Chippewa River Valley, Wisconsin

*"I'm like Will Rogers.
You know how Will Rogers never
met a man he didn't like?
Well, I never met an old tractor
I didn't like."*

—Harlan Johnson, tractor collector

Wisconsin Tractor Collector's Yard

Central Wisconsin

"Long about the first of February a certain sense of futility creeps in—you start talking about selling the ranch, or, failing that, giving it to someone you can't stand."

—Ralph Beer, *In These Hills*

Near Kraryville, New York
This tractor rests one-half mile from
Hughes Bultaco's shop, where Bultaco
restores motorcycles and sells Bultaco parts.
Jeff Hackett photo

CHAPTER 4

Exodus

"The more a man can achieve, the more he may be certain that the devil will inhabit a part of his creation."

—Norman Mailer, *The Presidential Papers* preface

In the postwar era, the tractor truly replaced the animal as the source of power on the farm. New methods enabled the farmer to produce more in less time. In 1850, a farmer spent about 80 hours working 2.5 acres to produce 100 bushels of corn. By 1940, that farmer could produce 100 bushels of corn in 20 hours off that same plot of land. By 1975, those 100 bushels could be produced in about 3 hours on just over an acre of land.

In 1850, the tools needed to produce this corn were a walking plow and a harrow used to groom the soil, and a pair of strong hands to plant and harvest the crop. In 1975, the farmer used a tractor, 5-bottom plow, 20-foot tandem disc, planter, 20-foot herbicide applicator, 12-foot self-propelled combine, and trucks. The result for both farmers was a hard life. The distinction comes in the reward for a good crop. In the 1850s, a good crop meant a full larder. Prices were a factor, but the primary use of farm goods was sustenance of the family.

The 1975 farmer's fate was in the hands of the market. Whether or not the family was able to harvest a good crop, the main determination of success came from prices. If demand was strong and prices were solid, the farmer did well. If not, a few payments might have to be missed. The new truck might get sold. The farmer, more likely than not, would eventually choose another lifestyle. Even if the farmer chose to work the land, the children typically left for other professions.

The 1975 farmer had all the luxuries of modern life. The family enjoyed electricity, a telephone, running water, a new truck, and maybe even a satellite dish. The 1975 farmer was also at the mercy of the mighty machine created by the industrial revolution. The famous independence and self-reliance that founded our country were transformed into something else. Compared to other small businesses, farming is a particularly hard choice. The hours are long and hard, vacations are hard to come by, and the start-up investment is significant. Many of the luxuries most of us take for granted disappear. No paid vacation. No sick time. No hanging out at the water cooler shooting the breeze about Monday night football or a coworker's new house.

All of this would be more tolerable if farming paid well. Take one look at many of the miserable professions people choose and the draw of a big salary is readily apparent. Operating a small farm did not pay terribly well through the 1960s and 1970s, and this continued to decline in the decades that followed. Almost 10 million people left the farm between 1950 and 1960, and the farming population shrank from 25.1 million to 15.6 million.

The farm became the mechanized operation envisioned by those who hoped to solve the "farm problem" in the 1920s and 1930s. The remaining farmers used modern machinery and methods to produce more crops from less land. The industrial revolution had indeed arrived on the farm. People left the farm in droves and were lured to the cities and growing suburbs to become bankers, doctors, engineers, teachers, and janitors. Anything that offered a reliable wage, health benefits, and tolerable work hours seemed a better choice to millions of the daughters and sons of rural America.

Wisconsin

*"My dad, he didn't believe in tractors. We always did everything with horses.
I had two brothers in the second world war. One stayed on the farm and he bought a 1936 A John Deere
along with a plow and cultivator. In 1949, my dad gave in and bought a brand-new John Deere
with plow and cultivator for $1,900."*

—Ervin Lewandoski, farmer and tractor collector

**Cascade Range Foothills,
Washington**

*This crawler is all that remains of a retired
construction equipment company.*

"He (the farmer) will stand on both
his feet—one foot on the soil for his
livelihood, and the other foot in industry
for the cash he needs."

—Henry Ford, *Ford News*, April 1936

Somerset, Wisconsin

Somerset, Wisconsin

"*For this is what America is all about. It is the uncrossed desert and the unclimbed ridge. It is the star that is not reached and the harvest that is sleeping in the unplowed ground.*"

—Lyndon B. Johnson, Inaugural Address, January 20, 1965

Old Farmstead, Utah

"Is not the vanishing agrarian the true heir of Western culture?"

—Victor Hanson, *Fields Without Dreams*

Just off Highway 29, Wisconsin

Near Willard, Wisconsin

This abandoned farm was found not far from my grandmother's home on a cold, clear March morning. The sun hung on the edge of the horizon, as full of promise as the cold ground emerging from the snow.

105

"*Maybe all one can do is hope to end up
with the right regrets.*"

—Arthur Miller, *The Ride Down Mount Morgan*

Central Wisconsin

CHAPTER 5

The Autumn of Rural America

*"It's still the country of the Future,
but it's also now the country of a rich, embracing Past."*

—Verlyn Klinkenborg, *The Rural Life*

By 1980, there were even fewer people on the farm. Stories of those who left or lost their farms are not hard to find. Ask around—you probably know someone who did one or the other.

In 1993, the U.S. Census stopped counting the number of people living on the farm. Wendell Berry, an eloquent writer with the voice of a poet and the soul of an activist, had this to say about the implications of the census change:

> American farmers, who over the years have wondered whether or not they counted, may now put their minds at rest: they do not count. They have become statistically insignificant.

The rural way of life is not dead, but the numbers of people living the remains of the dream that founded this country are no longer even counted. What we have is a new society based on the blood and sweat of our hardworking ancestors. The ideals that founded this country remain strong forces in America. The belief that you can pull yourself up by your bootstraps still exists in young and old alike.

Writer J. B. Jackson postulated that the prevalence of finely manicured lawns in America is nothing more than a nod of the hat to our agrarian roots, an attempt to re-create a little piece of the pastures that once surrounded our homes. A valid point, especially if you consider how little time is available in modern society and how much of that precious time is devoted to grooming, spraying, and landscaping tiny plots of ground. Jackson wrote about how the condition of the lawn is a status symbol:

> By common consent, the appearance of a front yard, its neatness and luxuriance, is an index of the taste and enterprise of the family who owns it. Weeds and dead limbs are a disgrace, and the man who rakes and waters and clips after work is usually held to be a good citizen.

Being a good citizen in America is more than just taking care of your lawn, but Jackson has touched upon a fundamental American ethic—hard work. Here in the Midwest, the work ethic is strong and prevalent. Rise early and work long hours to succeed. Stand on your own two feet. I see this ethic in the people I work with every day. They work hard and put in long hours, most not for personal gain, but simply because that is what they know. I see that work ethic in my family members. From farming the rocky soil of Slovenia to scratching out a hard living in the undeveloped land of central Wisconsin, our roots lie on the farm. Hard work was not an ethic back then, it was a matter of survival. That instinct carried through our family, from my 86-year-old grandmother's immaculate house to my 30-year-old sister's scrupulous care of her family.

Americans still value the hard work that founded this country, and I believe this value will carry throughout our nation's history. Even the dream of going West still has a little of the old magic, and people flock to Colorado, California, and other western states to hopefully make their dreams a reality. The romanticism of rural life remains strong. The dream of living in a pastoral setting draws more and more people in, and the fastest-growing portions of America's metropolitan areas are the so-called satellite communities.

Farm fields are being bought for ludicrous prices, outfitted with curving paved streets, walking paths, given names like Green Gables or Shady Brook, and then subdivided into small lots and filled with cookie-cutter homes. The new American Dream, for many, is three acres of a former cornfield filled with a brand-new ranch home with a view of more brand-new ranch homes. The well-off buy five acres right next to the pond that was dynamited in by the developer, and are surrounded by brand-new luxury homes and six-stall garages.

Hobby farms are also a hot commodity in the American twenty-first century. Move out to the country where you can raise horses, own a spread, and pay someone to mow three acres of grass with your brand-new John Deere compact tractor. The true country enthusiast may even cut his or her own firewood (for the fireplace in the great room), build a smoker (useful for smoking salmon and guinea hens when entertaining), or perhaps even "farm" a little plot of herbs, vegetables, and Japanese trees.

These new country lives are little more than the suburbs coming to roost a bit further afield, and the folks that live there often suffer from an odd community disconnect. Their friends are typically still in the city, and the new town, subdivision, or whatever you like to call it, is little more than a tract of land filled with beds and parking spots.

The social, professional, and cultural lives of the people who reside in an outlying community are often found in urban areas, but that pastoral setting is all their own. After a long of week of commuting to work in the city, our Nouveau Ruralites wake up on Saturday morning to brew some cappucino, take in the deer in the front yard, and then pack up the minivan and spend the day visiting friends or taking in the new art exhibit in the city.

Our true agrarian roots were hardly air-conditioned and satellite fed. The rural ideal that America was founded upon was based on a very hard life. Yes, those people were closer to the land, but the notion that they had a stronger value system is patently ridiculous. They had a harder life. They had fewer choices. Hell, these people did not have time to sin. If the larder wasn't full come November, the family would starve. If they didn't work hard and keep their nose to the grindstone, they would die.

The sweat and blood of our ancestors have become the leisure time activities of the populace today. Yes, people still crush apples to make cider, stuff their own sausage, and cut their own wood. My family does all of these things, and I treasure each task dearly, but such diversions are no longer part of a way of life. They are a pleasure and a family tradition.

Culturally, there is a longing for that lost way of life. Those people who move out to landscaped corn fields probably seek it, and many of the people who live in the remote corners of the country have found it.

The incredible rise in the popularity to restore and collect old tractors is also evidence of an interest in the past. Tractors in the pasture are becoming harder and harder to find thanks to the efforts of a nation of people that scoop up these relics and bring them back to life as running machinery, repainted work vehicles, or finely crafted recreations that look fresh off the factory line.

The popularity of some of the writers quoted in this book are evidence of this longing, as well. These writers understand that the loss of the farm has left a cultural hole. I believe, as they do, that we will find a way to fill this hole.

In the meantime, we have old tractors rotting away in fields to remind us of a way of life many of us don't even know we miss.

"We need places in reach of every community where children can imagine the prehistoric and the beginning of history: the unknown, the trackless, the first comers."

—Wendell Berry, *The Unsettling of America*

The Ozarks, Arkansas

The Ozarks, Arkansas

Turquoise Mine, Mojave Desert
Uwe Dietmer, the owner of a motorcycle travel company, took me to this struggling mine in California. The owners of the mine lived in a battered trailer down the mountain. Abandoned equipment was scattered all over the mine and the owner's yard.

Near Sarpy Creek, Montana
Clarke Sutphin photo

116

"But the care of our earth is our most ancient and most worthy and, after all, our most pleasing responsibility. To cherish what remains of it, and to foster its renewal, is our only legitimate hope."

—Wendell Berry, *The Unsettling of America*

Ghost Farm, Wisconsin

Augusta, Wisconsin

"There's no bigger thrill than bringing a junk pile back to life."

—Farmer Wayne Gamm, in an article in *Successful Farming*

Nameless Pasture, Wisconsin

119

"Some fields were still covered with an autumnal thatch, while others had spring so green that I almost longed to be put out to pasture."

—Verlyn Klinkenborg, *The Rural Life*

Maui, Hawaii

Kauai, Hawaii

Ozark National Forest, Arkansas

Somerset, Wisconsin

The number of people working on farms continues to shrink in the twenty-first century. Statistics are hard to come by because the U.S. Census Bureau stopped counting the farm population in 1993.

Whispers

"Who would not trade check, pension, and health care to leave his neon abode for a night-time ride on the tractor behind the garage, rabbit, fox, and great-horned owl paying their due as they race you for a furlong or two?"

—Victor Hanson, *Fields Without Dreams*

Farmers of the mid-1800s had very few choices. If they wanted to live, they tended their gardens, fed the animals, and built fences and barns and houses. When they woke up on Sunday morning, their decisions were pretty much dictated by their environment.

Today, many of us wake up on Sunday morning with the luxury of choice. We don't believe we have it at times—we have to go see this person or attend that function—but we do have choices.

One of the most rewarding choices I can make is to spend time in nature. My response is the strongest in parts of the world nearly untouched by civilization. I found it in the vast barren lands of the Australian Outback, where a farmer can be 50 miles from home and still be on his or her own land. That vast expanse of land virtually unchanged by man and absolutely untouched by modern civilization has an allure that is more than a pleasure; it is an essential piece of my soul.

Similar stirrings have come for me in the stretches of virgin Amazon jungle in Bolivia, on a tropical rural home in the Dominican Republic, and in the sleepy hills of the Ozarks in Arkansas.

Off Highway 12, Wisconsin

These emotional responses are hardly limited to exotic or untouched lands. I can get a lift from a walk in the local nature preserve.

One of the places that evoke the strongest response for me is driving, riding, or walking the farmlands and oak forests of my native Wisconsin. When I pass the Big Pine, the Rabbit Tree, or other landmarks that have been known only to my family and intimate friends for decades, a song of familiarity resonates within my bones.

There is a clearing in those woods where three poplar trees grow from a single source. In that tree, my grandfather, my father, and I built a deer stand. We nailed up a board ladder and built a wood platform about 15 feet off the ground. The stand was about 50 yards off of the end of one of the trails my grandfather had cut into his woods with a bulldozer.

Deer hunting starts with the light, and hunters are on their stands before light breaks. In order to use that stand, I had to walk into the woods in the dark. In the dark of predawn, it was easy to follow my grandfather's dozer-cut. I carried a flashlight, but more often than not, I turned it off and let my eyes adjust to the dark.

When I came to the end of the road, I had to veer off through 50 yards of brush to find the stand. This can be tricky, because one part of the woods in the dark looks pretty much the same as any other patch of woods 50, 100, or 1,000 yards away from your stand.

Lake Elmo, Minnesota

124

**Grandpa's Woods,
Willard, Wisconsin**

My grandfather's tractor one of the last times we used it. We cut up and split a giant fallen oak tree. The tractor wouldn't start, and we let it sit out next to our woodpile for a couple of weeks. We got the tractor started a few weeks later and drove it into the shed. The Ford has sat there ever since.

After getting mixed up on the way to the stand, I learned that if I start off the trail at a set point and just let my feet take me, I'll naturally come to the stand. Some hunters use ribbons or reflective thumbtacks on the trees, but I learned the trust-your-gut method. It's satisfying as hell, and it works.

The stand eventually fell down or was cut down—I forget which. That was more than 20 years ago and Grandpa's old road is long gone, but I can still find the heap of boards that was my first buck stand. It isn't always easy, and I can't tell you exactly how it is I can get there, but if I go into that old stretch of woods and follow my feet, they get me to the stand.

Just as your memory has a way of sensing place in the woods, I believe your soul can lead you to the right path if you have the courage to listen. A friend of mine says the Universe whispers to you. I believe he's talking about the same thing.

Those riffs I feel when walking in native woods, far-off jungles, and domestic mountains are reminding me that the most meaningful parts of life are found far from the urban McSociety that has nearly overgrown our world.

For the farmers who founded our country, that connection was a natural part of life. Working the earth was not a pleasure, it was part of the daily routine.

For much of America, spending time in nature is no longer part of the daily or even the weekly routine. And small friendly communities have given way to large cities.

"I have always looked upon decay as being just as wonderful and rich an expression of life as growth."

—Henry Miller, *The Tropic of Cancer*

Pine Lake, Wisconsin

When I took this photograph from my Old Town canoe, this turn-of-the-century pegged barn was starting to collapse and sag. The barn has since been bought by a couple from Minneapolis who have shored up the foundation, fixed the roof, and built a white two-story house downhill from the barn.

That loss, I believe, is a key aspect of the attraction of an old farm tractor that rusts away in a back lot or pasture. Our souls are tickled with the sense that something, somehow is missing from life. That old machine is physical evidence of that loss, a weathered fossil of days past.

I believe we need to listen to the those ticklings and find the strength to turn the whispers of the Universe into voices, and the voices into deeds, and the deeds into a world that makes sense.

Next time you see an old piece of equipment at rest on a fencerow or back pasture, stop for a minute, take in the beauty of the season and the land, and just listen. Maybe the Universe will whisper in your ear the way it did in mine.

126

ACKNOWLEDGMENTS

Thanks are in order to those who helped bring this book to life. First off, thanks to the friends and family members I roped into going old tractor hunting with me: Sam and Anna Wheeler, who spotted several gems in the Seattle area and planted seeds for the manuscript; Dave and Laurel Linner, who spotted the Colorado River Farmall; Warwick Schuberg, who spotted the Australian Farmall M; Mark and Jeff for help tractor hunting in Arkansas; my sister Amy and my favorite nieces, Hannah and Heather; Amy, Schekky, and Tom for spotting a couple of gems on the road to BEA; and to Darwin and Kent, for the North Dakota double-deer adventure finds.

I'd also like to thank those who provided photographs and information: Clarke Sutphin; Martin Pavey and Andrew Gibb, of the Leeds, UK tractor club; Jeff Hackett; The Wisconsin Historical Society; the Minnesota Historical Society; and Guy Fay.

To the gang from Cheryl Reed's writing class (Nikki, Julie, Vicki, Kelly, Becky, Anne, and Denise), whose enthusiasm for an early draft of the introduction helped me get fired up to write this (and the after-class beer sessions at Maxwell's didn't hurt the process, either). To Bev the Lawn Angel, for helping out with my leaf-covered lawn at the perfect time and supplying a couple of meals when I was too frazzled to cook. To my family and friends, thanks for your support, encouragement, and willingness to read my stuff! And, of course, to Darwinistan residents, allies, and nobility—thanks for all the Good Times.

I'd like to thank the people at Motorbooks who participated in the process: editor Darwin Holmstrom, for encouragement, support, and several key suggestions that greatly improved the book; editor Amy Glaser for her sharp eye copyediting, keen understanding of the topic, and helpful suggestions for writers to quote; editor Peter Schletty for shepherding the book through the final stages; designer Tom Heffron for his elegant cover and interior design; art director Becky Pagel for her support and tireless dedication to making good books; designer LeAnn Kuhlmann for her careful layout of the book; VP Zack Miller for getting me into this business and VP Tim Parker for being understanding enough to keep me doing it; managing editor Joe Bonyata for his attention to detail and publishing knowledge; and to sales rep Jason DeJoode, who provided several articles that are quoted in the book. Beers are on me at the next happy hour.

Last but not least: kudos are due to Koharski, whom you can always count on in a pinch.